Fall

Julie Murray

Abdo
SEASONS
Kids

abdopublishing.com

Published by Abdo Kids, a division of ABDO, PO Box 398166, Minneapolis, Minnesota 55439.
Copyright © 2016 by Abdo Consulting Group, Inc. International copyrights reserved in all countries.
No part of this book may be reproduced in any form without written permission from the publisher.

Printed in the United States of America, North Mankato, Minnesota.

052015

092015

 THIS BOOK CONTAINS
RECYCLED MATERIALS

Photo Credits: iStock, Shutterstock

Production Contributors: Teddy Borth, Jennie Forsberg, Grace Hansen

Design Contributors: Candice Keimig, Dorothy Toth

Library of Congress Control Number: 2014958554

Cataloging-in-Publication Data

Murray, Julie.

 Fall / Julie Murray.

   p. cm. -- (Seasons)

ISBN 978-1-62970-919-2

Includes index.

1. Fall--Juvenile literature. 2. Seasons¬--Juvenile literature.   I. Title.

508.2--dc23

                    2014958554

Table of Contents

Fall. 4

Fall Fun 22

Glossary. 23

Index 24

Abdo Kids Code. 24

Fall

Fall is one of the four seasons.

Spring

Summer

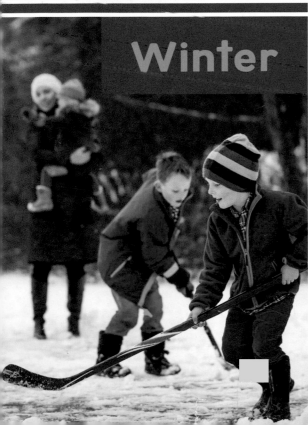

Winter

Fall

5

The air gets colder in Fall.

The days get shorter.

Leaves turn colors.

Some turn yellow.

Others turn orange or red.

Leaves fall to the ground.

Josh rakes the leaves.

Animals prepare for winter.

Squirrels **gather** food.

Geese fly south.

Bears eat a lot!

Pumpkins are **carved**.

Ellie helps her dad.

Apples are **picked**.

Aya loves apple pie!

What will you do this fall?

Fall Fun

build a bonfire

go apple picking

carve pumpkins

jump in a pile of leaves

Glossary

carve
to cut something into the shape that you want it to be.

gather
to bring together from many places.

pick
to gather by plucking.

Index

activities 10, 16, 18

animals 12, 14

apple picking 18

cold 6

daylight 6

plants 8, 10

pumpkin carving 16

abdokids.com

Use this code to log on to abdokids.com and access crafts, games, videos, and more!

Abdo Kids Code:
SFK9192

24